The Storied Agate

100 UNIQUE LAKE SUPERIOR AGATES

D1518480

by James Magnuson

Photography by Carol Wood

Adventure Publications, Inc.
Cambridge, Minnesota

Jas G. Mag

CAROL WOOD

Dedication

To our families, who enjoy agates and understand the joy they bring us.

To our siblings, who are slowly catching agate fever.

And to our mother, who likes anything we bring home (still).

Edited by Brett Ortler
Cover and book designed by Jonathan Norberg

10 9 8 7 6 5 4 3 2 1

Published by Adventure Publications, Inc.
820 Cleveland Street South
Cambridge, MN 55008
1-800-678-7006
www.adventurepublications.net
Printed in China
ISBN: 978-1-59193-309-0

The Storied Agate

100 UNIQUE LAKE SUPERIOR AGATES

Introduction

A feast for the eyes awaits you. You don't need to know anything about rocks and minerals or have any desire to hunt or collect them in order to delight in the natural beauty of Lake Superior Agates. These gems are wonderfully diverse and colorful and they are lovers of light. In this book we have captured all of these qualities and let the stones speak for themselves. You will see many varied types of Lake Superior Agates, some of which will have you asking if they are truly Lakers. (They are!) We have also included short and colorful anecdotes about when they were found and tips to help you find your own Lake Superior Agates.

This book is not a textbook and is only educational in the sense that you will see what natural forces are capable of producing. Here we provide a simple and non-scientific context on the natural processes that formed and then distributed these gemstones; some refer to this as a story of fire and ice.

First, the fire. Over one billion years ago the Lake Superior basin was formed by massive lava flows. Inside the cooling lava, air pockets were formed—most no larger than a pea but some much larger. Over hundreds of millions of years, fissures (cracks) formed in the cooled lava. As silica (quartz) liquids flowed through the fissures, the air pockets were slowly filled, and the liquid hardened slowly, one layer at a time. These layers are commonly known as fortifications. The most common Lake Superior Agates are fortification agates—gemstones with concentric, patterned rings. There are many other kinds of Lakers—eye agates, tube agates, moss agates, and so on. We will feature some of these additional agate types in this book, but we will focus on the stones themselves, instead of details about how each variety formed. We will let that remain part of the mystery.

So now you have a basic idea of how these beautiful stones were formed. Agates may have formed because of fire, but they are widely distributed thanks to the ice. Over hundreds of millions of years, the lava crumbled and the much harder silica-based agates weathered out of the host stone. The ice ages that occurred—some only tens of thousands of years ago—bulldozed hundreds of millions of tons of sand, dirt and stone and pushed this payload across the Upper Midwestern landscape. As the ice sheets receded, massive deposits of glacial till were left at the surface level in large, dense pockets. Running water, mostly in the form of rivers, distributed these glacial deposits even more, pushing some materials all the way to the Gulf of Mexico.

Maybe this book will spur some of you to go on your own hunt—in the wild, in a local rock shop or a museum, or online. Our primary aim in this book is for you to have an authentic experience and for you to behold the beautiful and calming qualities of Lake Superior Agates. Of all the gemstones on Earth, these are indeed some of the most accessible. Share this book with your children and your grandchildren, teach them to love and appreciate natural beauty, and possibly spark an interest in them to find their own treasures in the real world. Go with them and enjoy your time together. Whatever you find, you will remember it together and it will be something that is uniquely yours.

Madeline Island

HERE IS ONE of the classiest agates I ever found—I call it the "Bowtie Agate" because of the symmetrical bright white lines that divide the face of the rock. They say that the best things come in small packages. This little zinger is a gem that I prize just as much as the trophy agates that some hunters strictly focus on pursuing. There are many days when I'll spend my last hour looking for smaller agates and it's rare that I go unrewarded.

Bowtie

Holy Grail

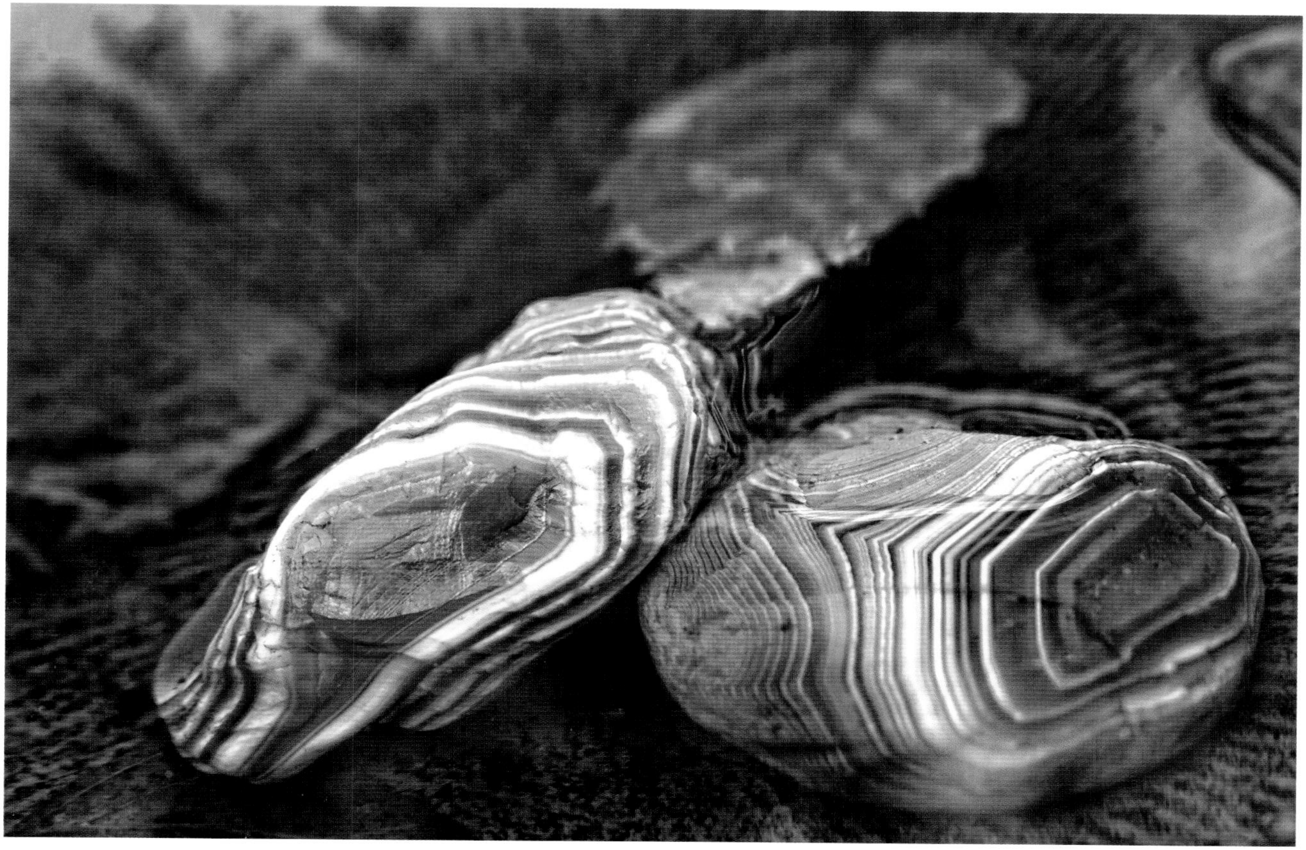

Fall Guys

IT IS OFTEN said that Lake Superior Agates love light. This small gemstone bears witness to this fact. Bring this stone into full sunlight and you will be astonished by all of the patterns that surround the surface. You will see dancing "shadows" as you look at its tight lines of bands and slowly tilt the rock from side to side. This agate is nearly colorless—it is simple and elegant, a jewel of nature for our wonderment.

Geometry 101

Colonel Mustard

A River Runs Through It

SPRING IS the best time of year for agate picking in farm fields. In the Upper Midwest, new rocks come up from beneath the surface every spring—giving rise to the term "winter potatoes." (Notice the "back" side of this beauty; it is a virtual baking potato!) After a few good rains, these "potatoes" are cleaned and ripe for the picking. There are a couple of good things about picking in farm fields—you can walk the nice straight rows that have been plowed to keep track of where you've been, and you get occasional visits from geese, pheasants and other wildlife.

Rock of Ages

Apollo

Lines of Resistance

"PAINT AGATES" are another rare form of agate. These stones are often distinguished by their very tight, intricate banding patterns and by bright or burnt orange hues (as opposed to the deep reds found in most agates), with alternating pastel-colored bands. These bands can be blue, green, yellow or purple. Tumble polishing paint agates often results in picturesque patterns emerging from the extremely intricate banding patterns. This paint stone is an absolute "knee-knocker." As I walked into a gravel pit one morning, I went past a pile of stones near the front gate that I (and several other agate hunters) had been over many times before, but I still scanned it as I went past. There sat a brilliant paint stone that contains three separate, distinctively beautiful faces—one that exhibits orange, red-green and blue, a second that displays tight orange-and-black bands and a third with peeling layers.

Grand Canyon

Madrid

Camo

SPRING IS an exciting time for agate hunters— especially in the Upper
Midwest where we are cooped up for about six months of the year. The winter
break gives us time to sort out good-quality gemstones from "garden rock," to
do some finishing such as tumble polishing or face polishing and to work on
creating displays for prized specimens. By spring, there has been a tremendous
amount of earth and gravel turnover due to freezing, thawing and melting,
and this exposes the top layer of stones. This agate is one I refer to as the
"snow agate." I took a chance one early spring day when there were still patchy
areas of snow covering the ground. The sun was shining and it was a warm
60 degrees, so I didn't expect much more than a winter sunburn. I found a
south-facing section of a large gravel pit that was mostly clear of snow and
began working the muddy hillside when I noticed a large number of stones that
had rolled down the hill and settled on the unmelted snow. As I walked the base
of the hill I quickly spotted this bright red-and-white agate. Nestled in the
snow was a perfect invitation to a new and promising season.

Mardi Gras

Piece of Cake

Dizzy

MANY SERIOUS agate hunters will tell you that a significant percentage of their best finds come in the first or last half-hour of the hunting day. "Walk off agates" account for many of the latter group, but it's not as easy to account for all of the agates found early on in the hunt. I drove into a gravel pit one morning and parked next to a pile of nice-sized stones. I walked over to the pile, looked up to the top, and saw what was obviously a nice-sized agate. This beautifully symmetrical Laker with a deep red center core is one of my top-o'-the-morning treasures.

Power Ball

Oh Canada!

Painter's Palette

IT'S SUITABLE THAT my sister chose to photograph this striking gem nestled among chain links. The conventional wisdom within the agate hunting community is to always ask for permission before hunting agates on someone else's land. Unfortunately, it's often difficult or impossible to locate landowners of gravel pits and there are fewer and fewer gravel pit owners that allow agate hunting due to concerns of legal liability or vandalism. This was the case when some family members visited Minnesota for my son's graduation. We were anxious to go out collecting, but pressed for time, we headed to a local gravel pit where the gates were open. We drove in, parked the car near the entrance, and dispersed to begin the hunt. After a couple of productive hours, we assembled to share our finds; this agate was undoubtedly the stand-out of the group. We decided to call it a (good) day and headed back to the car. As we approached, we could see that the gate had been closed and deliberately chain locked! Panic set in and we brainstormed ideas. One of my sisters said she knew an alternate way out and convinced my other sister to drive her rental car down a rutted dirt-and-grass pathway through a farm field and behind several old buildings. After hitting bottom several times, we asked my sister if she was sure this was a way out and she gave a strong affirmation and said, "Keep going!" Shortly after, we were able to get out onto an access road and all breathed a sigh of relief. When we asked my sister later if she did indeed know the path would lead out, she gave a sly grin but didn't utter a word.

Amber Waves

Nautica

Mad Cow

THERE ARE A FEW hazards to agate hunting that I mention throughout this book; they include inclement weather, hillside collapses, slippery rock piles that one can easily tumble down, and even angry gravel pit owners or operators. From midsummer to fall, there is another hazard I refer to as "dead piles." These are gravel piles that have been sitting since spring without new material being added or any old material removed. Usually I won't hunt these piles because agate hunters have already worked them over. However, there are times when there just isn't much new material and I make the effort to work these piles by slowly climbing back and forth and pushing top layers downward. I have found some excellent agates this way, but it's a lot of effort and, in the case of this beautiful white and purple colored specimen, a bit of a thrill too. I had been working a pile for about 30 minutes and came across this find, which encouraged me to "keep going." Several minutes later as I shoved another layer of rocks down with my work boots, a swarm of wasps came pouring out of a nest, which encouraged me to "get going." I quickly stumbled off the pile and made a beeline for my vehicle!

Swashbuckler

For Spacious Skies

Fishers of Men

ONE MORNING I arrived early to my favorite hunting spot, only to find that two even-more-ambitious collectors had gotten there first and worked over the rock piles with new stones. Discouraged but not defeated, I went over to a dusty pile of rocks that hadn't been through the washing process yet. Patience is always the name of the game in hunting for rare gemstones—if you don't have it you might as well go home. After about 2 minutes of slowly traversing the dirty heap of stones, a bright white-on-red pattern burst through the dust and dispelled my gloom of being second on the scene.

indy

Apache

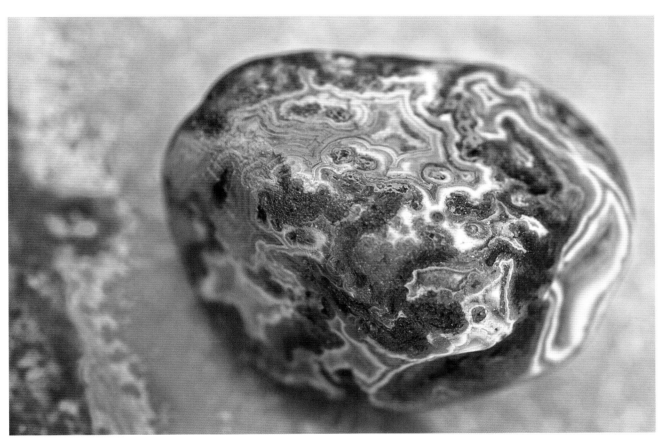

Material Girl

IT IS UNUSUAL when a husband and wife both have a passion for rock hounding. I think I can count on my hand the number of times I've actually gotten my wife to go out and hunt with me for more than 20 minutes at a time. On the other hand, she loves the beauty of Lake Superior Agates and always likes to see my finds at the end of the day and to pick out the premium gems. On one of our joint excursions, I was off climbing some rock piles for about an hour and realized that my wife's patience was probably waning, so I headed her way. She had been walking across the bottom of the rock pit, which was strewn with processed Lake Superior gravel. When she held out her hands and displayed her finds, this "killer agate" made me very proud, and I love to display it among my own best finds.

Ain't No Mountain High Enough

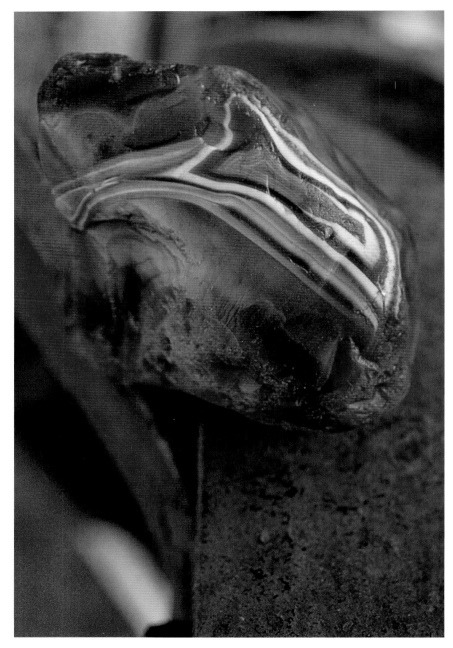

Ridge and Furrow

Leather and Lace

THIS PHOTOGRAPH shows two eye agates—one of the rarest types of Lake Superior Agates. Eye agates are almost always less than one ounce in weight, so if you are hunting for these, you need to be looking for smaller stones. These stones have "eyes"—bands in perfect concentric circles. Three dimensionally, the eye exists as a perfect hemisphere in the host banded agate, and the depth of the eye formation is therefore never more than the radius of the eye itself. Eyes can occur in varying degrees near the outside surface of any nodular, banded agate, and will sometimes occur along with more standard agate bands or "fortifications." The eye agate on the left is a stone that I found at the end of a long and fruitless day. It was sitting faceup in a sandy pile, and it was absolutely radiant, despite its diminutive size. This gemstone is a real eye-catcher!

Jeepers Creepers

Peace

El Sol

HERE'S ANOTHER agate that was found in a farm field. One of the draw-backs of picking in farm fields is that the cultivating blades can take a toll on the agates, splitting them into pieces, cracking them, etc. When I first found this agate, the unusual and beautiful colors gave me a jolt. As I cleaned the agate off, I could see that the damage done by the farm machinery would take some work to repair. Eliminating some of the worst breaks and fractures on this large gemstone wasn't easy; it took many hours on the rough grinding wheel of a face polishing machine, and a trip through the Stage One tumbling process to get a smoothed surface. Even when I can't restore a damaged top-shelf agate to a flawless presentation, I tell myself that I'd rather have a slightly blemished beauty than never to have found it. I think anyone would have a hard time parting with this gemstone.

Santa Fe

Better Half

Brownie Batter

WHAT DO YOU do when your daughter is enrolled in horse-riding lessons an hour away from your house? After you get tired of watching the first couple of sessions, you ask the trainer if there are any gravel pits or farm fields nearby. I was directed to a small private gravel pit about 2 miles from the stables and quickly determined that the newer rock piles were somewhat picked over. So I went toward the back part of the pit. I saw an unusual-looking stone on an old rock pile and picked up this amazing agate. This is by far the most intricate lacy-patterned tube agate that I have ever seen. RULE: Whenever you see something unusual, pick it up and look at it. I found a couple of other decent agates that day, but this stone was burning a hole in my pocket as I drove back to the stables. My daughter is the next biggest agate fanatic in our family and I know I've found something special when she feigns stealing one of my nice Lakers. She held onto this one for quite a while when I first showed it to her, and on several later occasions when going through my collection, she would slyly take it out and give me her "Who me, what are you talking about?" look.

Golden Eye

On the Horizon

Little Dipper

HERE IS AN AGATE that my daughter found for sale on a table at a sci-fi convention in Minneapolis. This is a one-pound "killer agate" that is easily worth several hundred dollars. The price tag fixed to the stone said $5. My daughter decided not to drive a hard bargain and just paid the named price. She did have to re-polish the face of the stone as the person who had first attempted it had done a bit of a rush job. My daughter has a particular skill with face polishing and when she was finished, the result was magnificent. Talk about a fantasy agate!

Gamer Face

Tan Line

Brainiac

THE NORTH SHORE of Lake Superior is generally inhospitable from mid-October to March. One January, we booked a family vacation at a lodge near Lutsen, Minnesota, to enjoy some winter activities such as skiing and snowshoeing. Unfortunately, that winter had one of the lowest levels of precipitation on record and we had to get a little more creative. One of the alternatives we found was hiking around the base of Gooseberry Falls, which had some awesome ice formations. We also got to walk the gravel-strewn beaches of Gitchee Gumee (the Native American name for "The Big Lake"). Despite the lack of snow, it was still plenty cold and there is always a stiff breeze coming off of Superior. I convinced my family to humor me and spend a little bit of time hunting for agates. Needless to say, we had the place to ourselves! Within 20 minutes, my wife and son packed it in and headed back to the car with the parting shot, "If you aren't back to the car in 15 minutes we're leaving without you." That put the pressure on for my daughter and me. We found a couple of agate pebbles and then, just as we were feeling the last grains of hourglass sand falling, we snagged this beauty and rescued it from the icy onslaught of winter storms to come.

Geometry 102

I Walk the Line

Crazy Horse

THIS IS A dual-chambered Lake Superior Agate; agates with more than one chamber are very rare. The larger chamber has a bluish hue with some pink and red fortification lines, and there is a smaller deep-red chamber. When my sister showed this photo to my brother from Florida who owns a bait shop on the Gulf of Mexico, he declared it the "Jaws!" agate.

You're Gonna Need a Bigger Boat

From the Chippewa on Down

A Feather in My Cap

THIS LITTLE PIECE of Lake Superior "Candy" gives a great illustration of the concept of fortification bands. The richness of color and the multiple concentric bands make this agate shine. One of the top online sellers of Lakers likes to put together a dozen or so small gems like this at Valentine's Day and Christmas and sell them as a "Box of Candy." This candy is sugar free, nonfattening, all natural and sure to please. Bet you can't "eat" just one!

Redwood Forest

Stetson

74

Prison Break

EVERYONE WHO IS passionate about their hobby will put up with all kinds of resistance in order to pursue their interests. In the case of this awesome 10-ounce classic black-and-white bander, the resistance came in the form of frigid temperatures and driving rain. Die-hard agate hunters will go out in the worst conditions—especially when there is rain because it means that there will be new stones exposed and cleaned. There was a pile of newly mined Lake Superior gravel at one of my favorite rock pits, so most of the stones were covered with mud and sand. As I slowly worked around the base of one rock pile, I could see just enough of this agate to observe the classic Lake Superior Agate surface pits to tip me off. Sitting in my van a few minutes later with the heater running, I was able to quietly admire this natural treasure. This agate has been face polished because the exposed surface was chipped during the gravel mining process.

Come Monday

ヲヲ

Over Easy

Crystal River

OVER THE YEARS I have met so many nice people at gravel pits, including pit owners and operators that often have stories of finding outstanding Lake Superior Agate specimens. There have been a few pit operators who have gone out of their way to help me by shifting around some of the stones. And then there are operators and owners who have no love for agate hunters. Usually this means they will brusquely ask you to leave and that's it. The agate pictured here is a half-pound beauty that I found when a loader operator saw me hunting at the bottom of a large gravel pile—and on his next two loads he dumped his load very near where I was standing. On the second load, I got out of the way just in time and as I looked down, there was this awesome agate. I decided not to press my luck and started to hike towards a different part of the gravel pit, not knowing whether I was just being paranoid or if the operator really did have me targeted. A few minutes later, my question was answered when he drove his machine up next to me and hollered out that if I wanted to hunt agates, I needed to ask him. Even though I had gotten permission from the landowner to hunt there, I decided not to argue, offered a short acknowledgment and headed to the exit with this nice prize.

Square Dance

Michigana

Solar System

"Children embarrassed by father picking up rocks
outside of fast food restaurant"

"Hotel guests seen searching for something in the landscape rocks"

THIS IS ONE of the agates I have found in the landscaping rocks at a local establishment—I don't remember which one. While the police never stopped me, my sister shared a St. Paul newspaper article with me that had a short story about a man who was hunting for agates in the landscaping rock at a local bank and was briefly apprehended and questioned. You will find plenty of quality gems anywhere in the Upper Midwest in landscaping rocks and along gravel roads. If your kids are 12 or younger, they will probably be right by your side. But once they hit that magic age, you are best to keep your public hunting escapades out of their purview.

Midnight at the Oasis

Totally Tubular

Mirage

HERE IS a trivia question for Lake Superior Agate lovers: What is one of the best rock shops in the world? Easy! It's called Agate City and it's located in Two Harbors, Minnesota. The specimens and displays shown at this store are truly phenomenal. Also, the store owner, Bob Lynch, is one of the most knowledgeable people about local mineralogy. The agate that is pictured in this photograph is one of only a couple of gemstones in this book that I purchased and it was ac-quired at Agate City. It is a truly magnificent paint agate, but it is a specific kind of agate: a Paradise Beach Agate. These are from an area near Two Harbors that bears the same name and where some of the most beautiful paint stones have been found. Agate City has a huge display case full of premium Paradise Beach Agates that I have spent hours gazing at. I could tell when I bought this stone that the owner was somewhat reluctant to part with it, despite having what is certainly one of the top five collections of Lakers in the world. If you ever find yourself in Duluth, Minnesota, Two Harbors is a leisurely forty-minute drive north along Lake Superior, and you will certainly find some treasures at Agate City that you will want to purchase for your own collection.

How Do You Like Me So Far?

Smoky and the Bandit

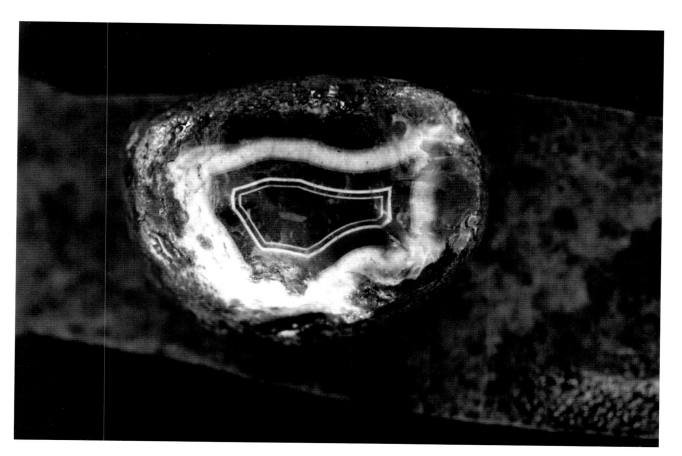

Paint it Brown

THIS AGATE IS another story of patience and persistence. There are so many days when I am unable to find hunting grounds with any substantial new material. This agate was found at a gravel pit that was completely dormant, i.e. mining operations had ended. But it wasn't a gravel pit that I had visited often so I decided to spend at least an hour giving it a once over. As I've mentioned before, a second or third pair of eyes will almost always find something new. There were a couple of gravel piles that had obviously been climbed on by other hunters, but I spent a little time on them anyway, and eventually found a few small agates worth keeping. I then started walking a section of the pit that had a layer of nice-sized rocks (mostly 6-12 ounces). I held scant hope of finding anything but began to walk a grid pattern that has proven successful in turning up agates among stones on the floor of a gravel pit. After about 20 minutes, I spotted this beautiful intact gemstone and felt well rewarded for making the extra effort.

Superior Bling

Hieroglyphics

Brown-eyed Girl

MY SISTER AND I have a habit of hunting together in some rather inclement conditions such as in a cold rain, in 90-degree baking sun with no shade, etc. We are also willing to climb up and down steep and slippery hillsides when there is quality new material at hand. Here's an agate that was found after my sister lost her footing and slid/tumbled down one such hillside. It was aptly named the "Sprained Agate."

Wax On

Roller Coaster

Cinnabun

ONE MORNING I arrived early at a large gravel pit that had been doing a lot of mining and processing. There were multiple large, new piles of clean stones and there was a group of women who had come out to hunt, working one of the piles with medium-to-large stones. So I started on one of the other piles and found several nice agates. A short while later the women came over by the pile I was on—and I had begun climbing up the pile after patiently working the base. One of the women commented that my climbing caused the top layer of rocks to slide down and "covered all the best rocks." The pile therefore would not be worth looking through anymore. Well, after almost ten years of agate hunting, I can confidently say that you never know where on the pile you might find the best agates and that a second or third set of eyes will often result in great finds. There is even a method to the madness of how to get the most mileage out of a gravel heap. I decided not to respond and instead quickly finished working the rock pile. I headed over to where the group of women had just been—knowing they hadn't climbed on their rock pile at all. This top-shelf tube agate is one of several quality Lake Superior Agates I found as I patiently worked the top, middle and bottom of the heap they left behind.

Niagara

Pulp Fiction

Egg Hunt

TRUE GEMSTONE hunters are always willing to take a measured risk. I had recently located a semi-active gravel pit and spoke with the owner about hunting for agates on his land. The gentleman had no problem with me being there, but warned me that he had cattle on his property and there was an aggressive bull in the herd. I affectionately called this gravel pit the "Bull Pit" from that day forward. One day after spending a couple of hours on the hunt and periodically casting an eye towards the grazing cattle, I found the agate pictured sticking out of a sand wall. Bull's-eye!

Bull's-Eye

Marley

Orange Crush

OUR FAMILY took a trip out east a couple of years ago and we were fortunate to connect with some old friends that had moved to the Washington, D.C., area. Over dinner, we shared some memories and talked about our current interests and pursuits. I often get odd looks when describing my passion for agate hunting. When my friend asked me a question about how big an agate has to be to have significant value, I said many of my best agates were about golf ball sized, to which he retorted, "Did you ever find one that said 'Titleist' on it?" We all got a good laugh out of that. Later that summer I was hunting agates in a farm field and found this nice specimen, which happens to be exactly the size of a golf ball. Not more than 10 minutes later I found a golf ball in the same field—likely the landowner's personal driving range. I had to laugh as I remembered the quip my friend had made.

Afterburner

Peachy

Half Moon

I HAVE BEEN lucky to share my passion for hunting Lake Superior Agates with my children. I have also been lucky to find some of my best agates while they were with me and to see them unearth some incredible specimens while by my side. My son, however, takes exception when we are hunting in close proximity with each other and I find a high quality gemstone. This monster (over 1 pound) beauty is one such find. When I picked up this big rock, it was very dusty and there was no pattern exposed, but when I cleaned it off, my son complained bitterly that I had stolen his agate. I have to admit that there is a competitive and territorial side to agate hunting, just like there is with other hobbies and sports. Luckily, I consider all of our finds to be "family property" and hope that they stay that way for many generations.

Big Water

Hallelujah

Walls of Jericho

I LIKE TO KEEP a small group of nice Lakers on my desk at work. People like to pick them up and look at them. On rare occasions they entice my visitors to ask about hunting for agates. There was a gentleman from India working in our office. We called him Ram (an abbreviation) and he took a particularly keen interest in these stones. Sensing his sincerity, we hit the agate trail early one Saturday morning. I took the time to show him a variety of rough specimens so that he was visually cued. Soon enough we were at the gravel pit and climbing some big and very muddy piles of glacial gravel. Per my instructions, Ram picked up anything he thought might be an agate and brought it to me for inspection, but no luck. Eventually I started bringing Ram over to me when I spotted an agate and let him "find" the agate so that he could see them mixed in with other stones. After a little while he stated, "I think I've got the hang of it," and started climbing up the side of a large rock pile. I went back to my own hunting and found this striking agate. Just as I was admiring my find, I heard a "wahoo!" and then a sliding and tumbling sound from the other side of the rock pile. I ran to the other side to find Ram on the ground laughing, covered with mud, and holding up a nice agate of his own. We finished off our hunting day and headed back home. I still hear from Ram occasionally; he is back in India, and we both get a big chuckle out of our day at the gravel pit.

Malibu

My Funny valentine

Freezer Burn

THIS IS AN AGATE that now belongs to my brother who owns a bait shop on the Gulf of Mexico. He has always shown an interest in my rock hounding hobby and one summer he even came north for a major agate hunting adventure in Fairburn, South Dakota, with my sister, a couple of the kids, and me. It was absolutely one of the best rock hunting experiences of my life and I could easily tell a dozen stories about our experiences in the Badlands, Grasslands and Black Hills of South Dakota. I named this eye agate the Fish Head Agate because of its uncanny resemblance to exactly that. At one family gathering, I was showing an assortment of recent finds to those that have an interest, and this was among them. I told my brother what I had named this agate and that it now belonged to him. He carries it with him every day, and since it's only about the size of a penny it aptly fits into the category of a "pocket pal."

Fish On!

Man in the Mirror

Class Reunion

ONE CHALLENGE of hunting for agates in the late summer is the infrequency of rain showers that clean off the rocks. Handheld spray bottles are not up to the task of cleaning large piles of gravel. I spotted a backpack weed and insecticide-spraying unit at a local hardware store and it occurred to me this could be filled with water and used to wet down rock piles. I'm pretty sure this idea was a result of agate lunacy. My kids said that when I exercised the pump handle I looked like one of those sci-fi show characters with a jetpack strapped to my back. I can't disagree but I have also had some great luck finding beautiful specimens this way. This nearly one-pound blue-and-dark-brown marbled gemstone is an example of an agate I absolutely would not have found if not for the backpack sprayer.

Pieces of Eight

Bermuda

Autobahn

I FOUND THIS one-pound agate that I affectionately call the "Horseshoe Agate" on an untouched pile of large stones that had been mined in late fall and then super-cleaned by late season rains, winter snow and melt off. I had the entire pile to myself on a bright, sunlit day and within 30 minutes on the pile I snagged this lucky agate.

Lucky Strike

Lava Gem

I Can See Right Through You

HERE IS A nice-sized agate with distinctive pitting, which is one of the characteristics that agate hunters key off of. Even when the stones are covered with dirt, if you see the right kind of dimpling or pitting, be sure to pick them up, clean them off and inspect. This agate was found at my favorite gravel pit in western Minnesota. What I love about this gravel pit is that they process their rocks in multiple stages, leaving many nice-sized stones that haven't been crushed or split. Also, the property owner is one of the nicest men you'll ever meet. He hasn't fallen victim to the fear of legal liability (in allowing agate collectors to come on his property). I gave this kindly gentleman a small amount of money when I met him. I think he was a bit taken aback, but I assured him that the enjoyment I got hunting agates in his gravel pit was worth many times what I gave him.

Holy Moly

Rock Candy

ROCKin in the USA

IN THE SPORT of baseball, a walk-off home run is a home run that ends the game—and the batter and his team walk off the field victorious. In the "sport" of agate hunting, we have what is known as the "walk-off agate." If it's towards the end of the day and you find a top-shelf gemstone, you walk off the hunting field victorious. It is the best way to end your day. This monster black-and-white beauty is striking, the ultimate walk-off Lake Superior Agate and it is a home run!

American Beauty

Fire and Ice

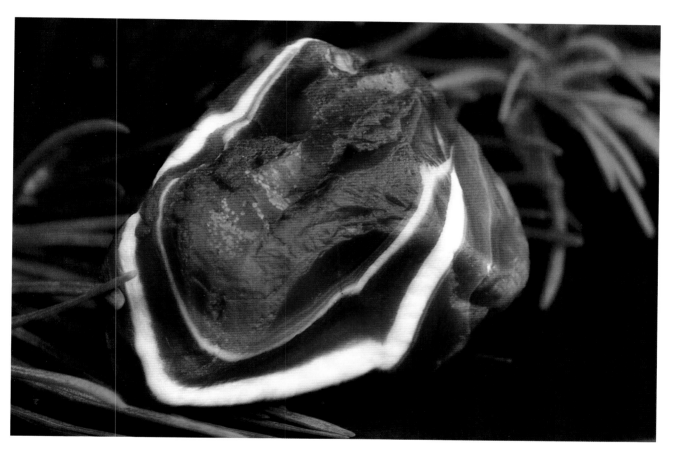

Coat of Arms

Featured Agate Varieties

 **Fortification agate:** The most common of all agate types, fortification agates feature multiple concentric bands with varying colors. Generally there are two alternating colors (such as red and white), but often there are several colors interspersed. Fortification agates with many colors, wide bands and striking "color separations" are more beautiful and valuable.

 **Tube agate:** Agates with stalactite-like tubes that either appear as linear features or in spiky patterns. Tube agates may result in bubble-like features on the top of an agate where the tubes have eroded more slowly than the rest of the agate material.

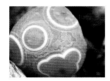 **Eye agate:** Agates with one or more perfect circular bands on the surface. These eyes are actually spheres that go deeper into the host agate material. The larger and more pronounced the eye, the more valuable the agate. There are also agates with concentric eyes (eyes inside of eyes).

 **Moss agate:** Agates with highly irregular banding patterns that are more lacy and interwoven than fortification bands, giving the appearance of moss. Moss agates will sometimes contain sections of well-organized fortifications.

 **Floater agate:** A silica or quartz-ball agate that features a fortification agate that is entirely surrounded by the host quartz material.

 **Water-level agate:** An agate that has bands that consist partially (or entirely) of parallel bands. It's theorized that the material in these agates may be heavier than in fortification agates and thus the bands formed at the bottom of the vesicle in the host rock.

 **Sagenite agate:** Agates with needle-like inclusions often in a radial, fan-shaped formation.

 **Shadow agate:** A fortification agate with extremely tight banding that, when held to light and moved back and forth, exhibits patterns of dancing shadows moving across the face of the agate.

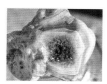 **Geode agate:** An agate that includes geode crystals in its interior. These may be white or gray quartz crystals, purple amethyst crystals, or dark smoky quartz crystals.

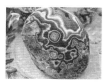 **Paint agate:** Agates that contain a broader range of colors than other agates, including bright orange, pastels (blue, yellow, pink, rose, green) and deep/rustic browns. These agates also have some of the most intricate banding.

 **Peeled agate:** Fortification layers that have been "peeled back" by uneven wind, water and ice erosion such that partial layers at the top have been removed.

About the Author

James Magnuson

As a young boy growing up in rural northern Illinois, Jim Magnuson spent much of his free time in the woods and fields hunting for wild nuts, berries and mushrooms, and also for fossils that were abundant in the limestone quarries and in creek beds. Of all these treasures from the earth, the fossils were his true passion and he would often come home, his pockets bulging with his latest finds. His mother lovingly referred to Jim as "Mr. Got Rocks." At one point when his collection began to overflow a corner of the basement, mom decided to stealthily dispose of some rocks that she knew were lower quality specimens. Jim still has the best fossils from his boyhood collection and occasionally brings them out for display.

For many years after leaving home Jim put his focus on developing his career as an Information Technology professional, first in Chicago, then Los Angeles, and eventually settling in central Minnesota. While working and raising two children, he had little time to pursue his own passions, but a trip to the shores of Lake Superior reignited an old flame. However, in northern and central Minnesota fossils are uncommon given that much of the surface level rock is lake-tumbled stone from the Lake Superior basin. Thus, Jim re-directed his focus to equally rare stones known as agates and set out to learn about and hunt for these beautiful gemstones.

Now Jim spends much of his free time in gravel pits, farm fields, and other outdoor locales where there are accumulations of Lake Superior gravel. He loves to share his hobby with family and friends and enjoys his outings most when he has someone along that is new to hunting Lakers that he can guide through the process of identifying agates in their true natural state. The earth is full of many treasures and Jim is always able to find peace through hunting, polishing and organizing for presentation, and giving away agates to those who find them interesting and beautiful.

About the Photographer

Carol Wood

While never able to create her own art, Carol Wood has always had a passion for the creative. She found photography to be the perfect outlet. Also from northern Illinois (Jim's sister), she still resides in the same locale and photographs everything from babies to, well, agates. It is more than a hobby for Carol, who makes photography her living since her departure from a career in banking.

Carol has attended photographic workshops and seminars across the United States. She strives for quality and originality—usually at the expense of her family's patience.

Jim introduced Carol and her family to the beauty of Lake Superior Agates many years ago, and she is an avid hunter when she has time to visit any location near the swath of glacial till. Her love of the stones, along with Jim's passion to share them, led to the idea for their new book, *The Storied Agate.*

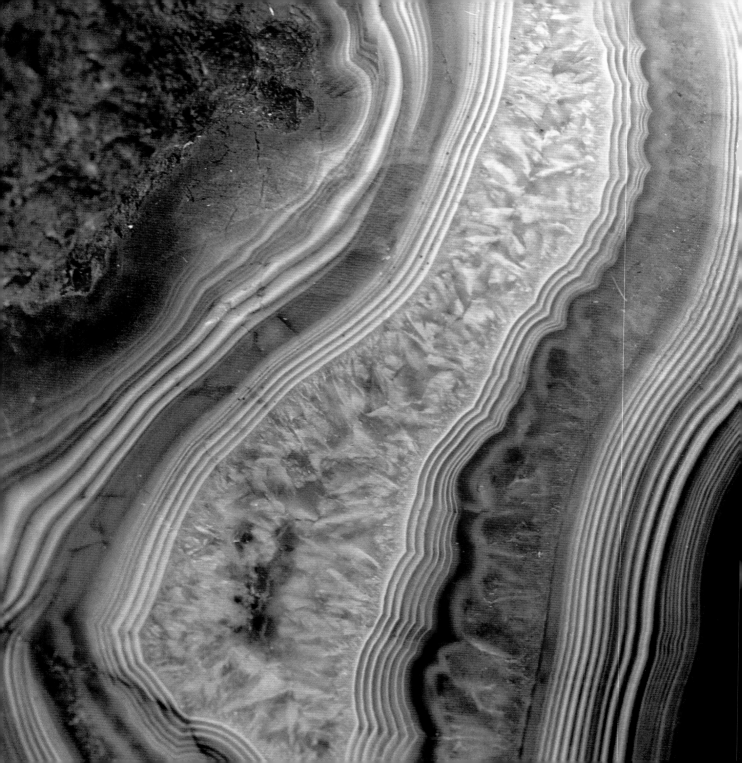